AFFIRMATIONS FOR H.E.R.

31-Day Devotional Journal

Wysdom Central Publications, LLC

"Igniting a Flame for God's Word & God's Wisdom"
Columbia, South Carolina

©2020, Ebony D. Green

Published by Wysdom Central Publications, LLC
Columbia, South Carolina
Email: wysdomcentralpubs@gmail.com

Editors: Business and Books, LLC & Wysdom Central Publications, LLC
Book cover design by Danny_media and jeweldsign
Printed in the United States of America

All rights reserved. No part of this publication may be reproduced, stored in a retrieval system, or transmitted in any form or by any means – for example, electronic, photocopy, recording-without prior written permission of the publisher. The only exception is brief quotations in printed reviews. Although the author and publisher have made every effort to ensure that the information in this book was correct at press time, the author and publisher do not assume and hereby disclaim any liability to any party for any loss, damage or disruption caused by errors or omissions, whether such errors or omissions result from negligence, accident, or any other cause.

By Permission. All definitions, unless otherwise indicated, are Used with permission from the Merriam-Webster Dictionary; Merriam-Webster.com. 2019.

Scriptures taken from the Holy Bible, New International Version®, NIV®. Copyright © 1973, 1978, 1984, 2011 by Biblica, Inc.™ Used by permission of Zondervan. All rights reserved worldwide. www.zondervan.com The "NIV" and "New International Version" are trademarks registered in the United States Patent and Trademark Office by Biblica, Inc.™

Scripture taken from the KJV are taken from the KING JAMES VERSION (KJV): KING JAMES VERSION, public domain.

Scripture quotations marked (NLT) are taken from the Holy Bible, New Living Translation, copyright ©1996, 2004, 2015 by Tyndale House Foundation. Used by permission of Tyndale House Publishers, a Division of Tyndale House Ministries, Carol Stream, Illinois 60188. All rights reserved.

Scripture taken from the New King James Version®. Copyright © 1982 by Thomas Nelson. Used by permission. All rights reserved.

Scripture taken from the Amplified Bible, Copyright © 1954, 1958, 1962, 1964, 1965, 1987 by The Lockman Foundation. Used by permission.

Unless otherwise indicated, all Scripture quotations are taken from THE MESSAGE, copyright © 1993, 2002, 2018 by Eugene H. Peterson. Used by permission of NavPress. All rights reserved. Represented by Tyndale House Publishers, a Division of Tyndale House Ministries.

Dedication

This book is dedicated to the Trinity for helping me find the innate deep treasure of H.E.R. and all the women You used as seeds in my journey. This book is also dedicated to women in pursuit of defeating a stuck place or cycle. For women who desire to know and discover "her" or their feminine selves as described by God and for those that seek to be affirmed in their true identity.
This book is for **H.E.R.**

Table of Contents

Introduction 7
H.E.R. Explained 9
Instructions 11
Day 1: "I am H.E.R." 13
Day 2: "Words shape our worlds" 17
Day 3: "Moving DO to DONE." 21
Day 4: "This season will not repeat" 27
Day 5: "The Power of Choice" 31
Day 6: "I am Committed" 37
Day 7: "Painstaking Pathway" 41
Day 8: God is my Refuge… 45
Day 9: "I am beyond a flower; I am a garden" 51
Day 10: GrOw is divinely connected to "GO" 55
Day 11: "Consider thy ways" 59
Day 12: "God's communication is love letters to me" 63
Day 13: "Accountability as the link from start to finish" 67
Day 14: "TRUST" 73
Day 15: SPEAK Open your mouth 79
Day 16: "Healing hands, Healing hugs,
and Healing conversations" 83

Day 17: "The God id of she/ her/ hers"
    Femininity in the eyes of God 87
Day 18: "Setting Place" 95
Day 19: Just A.S.K. HIM 99
Day 20: Masked Sender 103
Day 21: You've got GAINS! 107
Day 22: Be willing to be last. 111
Day 23: Do not discount spiritual seeds 115
Day 24: "Give it a name" 119
Day 25: The When/Win Situation 123
Day 26: The WAIT 127
Day 27: "Bit-by-Bit" 131
Day 28: "NOW" 135
Day 29: "NEVER give up!" 139
Day 30: Chosen vs. Frozen 145
Day 31: I am God's Businesswoman 149

Closing Thoughts 153

Introduction

By the time this book is released, I (Ebony D. Green) will be 34 years of age. Within these decades of life, I have changed careers twice, experienced the murder of someone close to me, seen people pronounced dead and brought back to life after praying for them, called off a "shiesty" engagement, obtained a few degrees, coached/counseled/prayed people through what I have yet to attain (but earnestly desired), questioned myself during difficult seasons, let go, failed a plethora of times, made even more mistakes, chose LIFE, walked/talked like a boss while screaming inside, looked back in regret too many times, realized passions, sinned and experienced forgiveness, and now redeemed, cried myself to sleep nightly only to get up and pray someone else through their low moments the very next morning, forgave, traveled to countries, realized my value, lived in multiple states, enjoyed a plethora of healing hands, hugs, and conversations with my loved ones, did what I knew not to do, lived in obscurity, realized why strangers are drawn to reveal their life stories to me in grocery stores especially and other public places, did it scared, did it without the full blueprint, did it with no one who did it before, learned to not shrink back, defeated the stuck place, discovered my identity in God, focused on perfecting the fruits of the Spirit and not solely His gifts, sworn into prestigious boards, obeyed the Father when it seemed to completely lack common sense, learned the Lord's voice, advocated for Christ in the marketplace, decided to trust Jesus and those He meant for me to trust, discovered the character of God, fought to be integral and keep the character of God, fell in love with the character of God, realized my purpose, embraced writing as a place of healing, passion, and discovery, delved deeper into the mysteries of Christ through the Bible, wrote numerous books no one has seen (this will be the first solo work), taught all cohorts in KINGdom business, intentionally treated the probono client the same as the millionaire status client, learned God and "chose" to draw closer daily, used my voice but did not love it more than His, poured into my beautiful God children, launched businesses and ministries, created a KINGdom business directory app, birthed businesses/ministries for others…just to share some of HER/MY experiences.

As a caveat, I have learned to appreciate each experience no matter the sentiment in that specific moment. I now know that many of those times were not solely about me but for future people that would be helped, encouraged, and ultimately grow all due to my life happenings.

It is not by happenstance that my first book is for women. So many women, younger and older have helped me through these seasons of life. It is only fair to give the treasure back but with even greater insight with the help of the precious Holy Ghost.

This book is for **H.E.R.**

H.E.R. Explained

Some years ago, the Lord shared that He wanted me to write a journal for women. I now realize it was a level of maturation that I needed before the release of the book but each life occurrence thereafter was affirming me into the woman He had designed. Life seasons i.e. 20s are often a finding place, 30s denote maturity and full growth, 40s are fulfillment years, 50s are typically the settlement into purpose, the 60s are notably filled with wisdom and reaching back to give back, while the 70s and beyond are Biblically the years of Grace. Even with the aforementioned moments in the introduction and many unspoken life experiences, this journal is being released by Grace because only God knows and can give ALL things. Simply stated, I have not had every life occurrence and can only share or impart wisdom fully by the Grace of God. God has divinely given me everything I needed for this journal to call H.E.R. forward. Take a peek into what He specifically shared with me.

The Spirit of the Lord said... *Chosen vs. Frozen. This journal will be ways to get unstuck no matter the season of life "she" is in. I will have to give great revelation for this because many experiences you have not had, will not have, have been protected from and others you will have later. Therefore, acknowledge openly, forwardly and from the start that the journal is divine and designed with H.E.R. in mind.*

This is for the woman that is getting unstuck. We are not meant to survive but LIVE and THRIVE. This 31-day devotional journal will walk you through 31 lessons, experiences, and divine revelation given by God that is necessary to call H.E.R. forth. If fully received and embraced, you will walk away with more of a voice and will no longer be stuck in realized or covert places. Life's vicissitudes have a way of making you feel like you are not the woman you were designed to be. These Affirmations are a prophetic calling divinely authored by Heaven to birth every Godly unique place in you as a woman.

Your assuredness, identity, and knowledge as a woman are guaranteed to thrive. H.E.R. is en route by way of Heaven. Divine woman come forth, rise, thrive, and live. Heaven has summoned you and the earth has need of your glory!

"H.E.R."

Heaven

En

Route

En route – "she" is on the way by way of HEAVEN.

Instructions

1. Read the Introduction and H.E.R. Explained.
2. Select 15 minutes *minimum* to read daily for 31 consecutive days.
3. Read the day's journal entry.
4. Say the affirmations **aloud**.
5. Write your own affirmation.

***For each journal day, visit the blog *H.E.R. Space* on www.ebonydgreen.com and share with other women your experience for that day. You can converse directly with the author at *God's Businesswoman* on Facebook and Instagram. Share what was your favorite day!

Day 1

"I am H.E.R."

Heaven

En

Route

En route – she is on the way by way of HEAVEN.

Journal themes~

HER identity shaped by God

Understanding God's identity and embracing His uniqueness for women helps thwart identity not from God i.e. alternative lifestyles. Be sure to know and more importantly understand why God created you as a woman. Embrace and appreciate what you bring to the table. This journal will explore the strengths, frailties and depths of *H.E.R.* There are so many attacks that are sent through "suggestion" of society about who a woman is. In reality, the only one who should define "H.E.R." is the one who created HER i.e. God.

HER words

Women's words have power to create what is not yet seen. That is the power of Godly femininity. Words from H.E.R. are influential and will either make or break generations, ask the first man, Adam. This is why this journal is committed to the imperative stance of aligning H.E.R. words with His. Through this affirmations journal, you will speak to the unseen and cause it to birth fully in your life.

HER femininity

Woman…Godly femininity, come forth! HEAVEN has summoned you. Prepare to take off into the design of who God created you to be. True femininity is divinely inspired. Today commences the journey of embracing the unique and Heavenly aroma of H.E.R.

He made HER on purpose!

He made a woman on purpose (Colossians 1:16). God…Heaven…this earth has need of you. The Lord uniquely made you. So, do not try to be anything other than…H.E.R.

H.E.R. (woman) is "en route" for many women because she needs to be awakened, her Godly designed femininity realized, questions ultimately answered, hurts responded to, and wounds/sears of the past nurtured.

> As a woman, anointed to speak to women,
> I call H.E.R. healed today; it begins in you.
> Embrace the essence of this journal and your life
> as a woman will forever be changed for the best!

DAY 1

TODAY'S AFFIRMATION

1. I am specially thought of and created by God.

2. I am not helpless but rather created to help through my insight, wit, as well as my ability to fill voids and provide wisdom.

3. I am created to do what men cannot (biologically) – I am woman. I happily embrace my created differentiation.

4. I am a natural producer and multiplier of all that I carry inside of me. I am a life-giver, what was once dead can live in and by me. Sperm alone is a seed, but in me, it has LIFE.

5. I am H.E.R. encompassed with all things good and God. I love it all!

WRITE YOUR OWN DAILY AFFIRMATION:

Day 2

"Words shape our worlds"

Proverbs 18:21

The tongue has the power of life and death, and those who love it will eat its fruit.

OH TO DECREE...

Words have literal power. Transparent moment, I can recall many times in my life where drama seemed to follow me. Or there was always something going on where I was the focal point. These occurrences persisted whether I initiated them or not. Drama in this context was not reality television worthy but it was beyond the usual vicissitudes of life. Frankly, I was ready for this theme to cease.

I was not oblivious that "I" was the common denominator. After prayer, I received a simple response:

"Your words shape your world."

This unpretentious statement shifted everything. I became more mindful of what I was giving life to via my words. Often times, we cannot control what we are presented with. However, our reactions, words and dispositions either eliminate or resurrect erroneous life consequences.

When I began to take inventory of my mental, verbal and non-verbal responses. I ultimately decided that I would control them no matter what was being presented; life subsequently changed for the better.

Now, I take each word, thought and expression, as I am either killing or giving life to someone or something with every release. This includes every greeting, smile, what I take time to listen to or what I decide to give my voice to.

My words either affirm or deny access for what is to come in my future. I have further learned that my presence and silence speak volumes. Many charged with accessory to crimes often regret what they affirmed with their presence, words and/or silence. There is a time to be present, a time to affirm and a time to be silent. Understanding that your verbal and non-verbal speaks, and giving consideration to all of them will shift the trajectory of your forward.

Affirmations. Decree and declaring. The power of words. God has always talked to me deeply about the words that I release. I am finding that the place of inception i.e. the mind is the greatest place of work. We have to begin with our thoughts, which will transform our speech and ultimately serve as an incubator for our verbal releases.

What are you feeding your mind? This spans from music to entertainment such as television. Also, relationships can often narrate or enhance what we rehearse mentally about ourselves. Regardless of the source, whatever you *feed* your mind, is what will be *released*. What is released is what you will ultimately *see* in your world.

Our lives *speak* one of two things: death or life. I can look around you, at your connections, progress over a period of time and know what your life speaks before you ever-utter one word. Today, let's make the right affirmations and begin well. This moment marks the day where we take all power back with our words. As a result, our lives will change for the better!

DAY 2

TODAY'S AFFIRMATION:

1. Today, I renounce any word (verbal & non-verbal) released by me, about or over me that has given meaning or authority to anything other than God's original design for my life.
2. I take back the authority of my verbal releases. I decree and declare that from this moment forward, I control what I give life to with my presence, my focus, and my speech.
3. I innately consider what I feed my mind as it shapes my releases and ultimately what and who will be seen in my life.
4. My words shape, not solely my world, but all of those assigned to me. As a result, I speak life and renewal to all things good and God.
5. I pray removal of everyone and everything that is not in alignment with this NEW world my words have thusly created today.

WRITE YOUR OWN DAILY AFFIRMATION:

Day 3

"Moving DO to DONE."

Mark 11:12-25

The next day as they were leaving Bethany, Jesus was hungry. Seeing in the distance a fig tree in leaf, he went to find out if it had any fruit. When he reached it, he found nothing but leaves, because it was not the season for figs. Then he said to the tree, "May no one ever eat fruit from you again." And his disciples heard him say it.

On reaching Jerusalem, Jesus entered the temple courts and began driving out those who were buying and selling there. He overturned the tables of the money changers and the benches of those selling doves, and would not allow anyone to carry merchandise through the temple courts. And as he taught them, he said, "Is it not written: 'My house will be called a house of prayer for all nations'[a]? But you have made it 'a den of robbers.'[b]"

The chief priests and the teachers of the law heard this and began looking for a way to kill him, for they feared him, because the whole crowd was amazed at his teaching.

When evening came, Jesus and his disciples[c] went out of the city.

> *In the morning, as they went along, they saw the fig tree withered from the roots. Peter remembered and said to Jesus, "Rabbi, look! The fig tree you cursed has withered!"*
>
> *"Have faith in God," Jesus answered. "Truly*[d] *I tell you, if anyone says to this mountain, 'Go, throw yourself into the sea,' and does not doubt in their heart but believes that what they say will happen, it will be done for them. Therefore I tell you, whatever you ask for in prayer, believe that you have received it, and it will be yours. And when you stand praying, if you hold anything against anyone, forgive them, so that your Father in heaven may forgive you your sins."*

I am analytical. However, I have found that analysis can become paralysis if we are not careful. All perfectionists stand up! These types often wrestle with the questions: *What should I do? Is this correct? Is this for the now? How do I get it done?* By the time your mind over works what you set out to do, the passage of time, stagnation, and lack of progress has manifested.

Women are intrinsically organizers; we pull things together in our homes and worlds. Recently, when I was doing a necessary purge in my home, I found a list I generated as a child.

It detailed every moment of my day, from showering, homework, who would visit, how long I would watch television to my time for bed. I have always been an organizer! To this very day, I make a to-do-list every morning. Within my company, people pay me to bring order to chaos in their businesses or general structure to their plans. Ordering, "doing," and organizing are all a part of my gifts. However, I noticed that my personal productivity was not where I wanted it to be. I needed help with moving my tasks from "just doing" to done.

The "do" is sometimes prayer, writing it out, getting instruction or advice from someone, working on some aspect of the instruction, creating time before the day ends to get it done. Oftentimes, working on a task instantly in some form brings on immediate change and progress towards what the Father has given.

What I am finding – when God gives a word, always do something with it.

The God that we serve is an ever-moving, always producing and always getting- it done God. Today's scripture details when Christ cursed the unproductive fig tree. When you are God's daughter, it is in your DNA to get it DONE. One wrong thought can serve as an eternal deterrent that prevents or delays your original to-do-list.

Satan cannot stop plans. However, he can try to cloud the mind with questions that are really masking internal fears.

One of my daily affirmations that I heard so clearly in my dreams one night was the voice of the Lord telling me this: *I know what to do and I do it quickly*. The Lord affirmed these words to me because I needed aid in my production. Now, I encourage you to pronounce these powerful words over your day, tackle something on your to-do-list and move it from simply doing to **DONE**.

TODAY'S AFFIRMATION

1. I decree and declare: "I know what to do and I do it quickly." I have clarity in my mind always. In all I do, I do it fully to the glory of God.

2. My mind is sound and it is filled with the power and love of Jesus Christ.

3. The spirit of fear, restlessness, procrastination and/or laziness is not a part of me.

4. I am a woman of daily progress. Every day I am fruitful and cause things to multiply.

5. Clarity exudes my speech, navigates all my ways and stabilizes me before God and man.

6. I am a daily producer. My productivity and innate gifting brings me forward and before great men.

7. Today, I am creating a realistic to-do-list that is in full alignment with my season and who God created me to be. I affirm proudly that I am moving from just "doing" to getting things done.

8. I start this day with a clearness of thought and internal action that causes great wealth to come to my hands.

9. I AM A FINISHER.

DAY 3

WRITE YOUR OWN DAILY AFFIRMATION:

Day 4

"This season will not repeat"

Ecclesiastes 3:1

There is a time for everything, and a season for every activity under the heavens…

Have you ever experienced a guest who overstayed his or her welcome? They used your things as though it belonged to them. They did not take the polite hints that it was time to leave. They extended the conversation and formulated reasons to remain. Or they went away for a short time only to somehow return for a longer stent than the previous one.

Some of you may be fortunate enough not to have experienced these types of guests. However, we do have life seasons that have overstayed their time or just seem to always come back. For you, it may be a relationship, a mentality or a financial status.

A strong indicator it is time for a new season is a climate change. Seasons often repeat or continue beyond their normal span when something is off kilter.

For instance too much or too little aluminum in the environment will begin to set things off with the climate.

You prevent seasons from having an extended stay or turning into a lifetime by discerning the season you are in. Certain relationships, mentalities or statuses do not have to be perpetual. You distinguish between seasons simply by asking the Father: what is this time for? Anything or anyone not in alignment with that season must be purged. For instance, coats are not for the summer. Nativity is not supposed to be a characteristic of adulthood.

If it is the "end" of a certain season (singlehood, raising children, young adulthood etc.), ask God what He desires for you to accomplish in that season. Be intentional with working on something daily regarding the time. You prevent the season from overstaying or returning by working on and completing the revelation He gives you for that time.

DAY 4

TODAY'S AFFIRMATION

1. I know what the day is for and I work diligently to accomplish every goal.
2. This is a season of _____. I will reach the apex of this season without hindrance or delay. Should an obstacle arise, I will ask God for the way to go around it.
3. I will not covet seasons that have past because I embrace all that God gives daily and press ahead.
4. Any person, thing or mentality that is not in alignment with this season is being purged today.
5. No seasons are repeating or extending as I focus daily to maintain balance and efficiency in every area of my life.

WRITE YOUR OWN DAILY AFFIRMATION:

Day 5

"The Power of Choice"

Galatians 5:13

You, my brothers and sisters, were called to be free. But do not use your freedom to indulge the flesh; rather, serve one another humbly in love.

Chosen. Choice surrounds us daily. We can choose salvation or not. The good eating versus bad eating option. Clothes, spouse, friends, career, or domicile. Choice is powerful because it determines your course. There are very few choices that you can take back once they are made. Our choices, right or wrong, brief or long carry an air of residue that marks us.

In some instances, the status of our health indicates the choices made. For some, the results of their choices become apparent immediately, others it waits until middle or advanced age to cause impact. Nonetheless, choice is powerful and we will reap what we sow.

Knowing the frailty of man since the beginning of time, God still has chosen us. He marked us as belonging to Him. He promised elevation for our future (for those that choose Him back). It feels good to be chosen. Because being chosen denotes several things.

Intentionality. God could have made another choice but He chose you. Some may think/believe there was/is a better choice but it does not matter because He chose you. Ephesians 1:4 states, "According as he hath chosen us in him before the foundation of the world, that we should be holy and without blame before him in love".

Selectivity. Exclusivity. The definition of exclusivity says "restriction" to a particular person. You are the only one that matters… YOU are God's choice. The King of Kings, Lord of Lords, the only true God, Alpha and Omega, omnipotent, omniscient, omnipresent God chose you.

Now how does that feel? It should render the 3rd point of what being chosen indicates: *LOVE*.

Love is a choice action. 1 Corinthians 13 describes love and they are all action words…something to intentionally do for or towards another. You do not have to love; it is a choice to be kind, long-suffering etcetera…

God does this for us. Being chosen, God's tangible love is felt upon our lives.

The power of choice is you do not have to do it but you do. The root of God choosing is love.

God choosing us should be the formula behind all of our choices in life, from food to friends. The choice should indicate *intentionality* and it needs to be rooted in *God's love*, not the construct that your soul (mind, will, emotions), culture or fluctuating feelings created. God chose us with such particularity, and *exclusivity* a NEW standard was created in how you should operate in what you choose to do, who you choose to love, or incorporate with generally.

DAY 5

The standard that being chosen creates is necessity of "showing up." You have to show up.... Be present in the decisions that are made. There is an understanding in some moments in time, you may not be able to be as present in your choosing as you like due to circumstances of the season. However, this cannot be an excuse. Do not allow seasons to turn into a lifetime. Not showing up, not being intentional, not changing even small things communicates a lack of value or care for the chosen, be it a thing or person.

In chosen relationships, this may breed and cause the chosen one to internalize rejection, abandonment or feelings of resentment. Not showing up in your choices can spark extreme contention and confusion.

In your chosen places, things, and relationships uphold a standard of care – by you showing up.

It is an age old saying to treat others the way you desire to be treated. Deal with others the way you desire to. Respond to people, places, and things the way you would like it reciprocated.

The power to choose and the benefit of being chosen should be a reconciled place. In other words, they should mirror God's initial model for all of our choices.

We know who and what we choose, and who and what we allow to choose us. These choices shape our lives for the good, bad, or indifferent.

Conflict in human choices will arise. We know this solely by being the chosen of God, at times, our lives contradicted being the chosen of the almighty God.

Raise the standard by beginning with you. Are you showing up in the process? Yes or No. If you are, then how? (Be intentional)

Are you valuing what your chosen is bringing (be it family, friend, or spouse)?

Showing up (presence) negates or trumps most contentions by solely being attentive to matters.

If you desire to end the scene of conflict in your "chosen" situations, places, and relationships, raise and become the standard. This is the power of choice.

TODAY'S AFFIRMATIONS:

1. Father, I thank You that I am the chosen of God and that daily I choose You back.
2. I understand Your formula of choice is marked by intentionality, exclusivity, and love.
3. I empower my now and all chosen relationships by emulating the above method in my walk.
4. When I hit a wall in my choices, I raise and become the standard of The Chosen.

Thank You God for choosing me and showing me Your way.

WRITE YOUR OWN DAILY AFFIRMATION:

Day 6

"I am Committed"

Mark 10:29-30

And Jesus answered and said, Verily I say unto you, There is no man that hath left house, or brethren, or sisters, or father, or mother, or wife, or children, or lands, for my sake, and the gospel's, But he shall receive an hundredfold now in this time, houses, and brethren, and sisters, and mothers, and children, and lands, with persecutions; and in the world to come eternal life.

Colossians 3:1-3 (paraphrased)

When you are in Christ, you commit to things above and not what is on the earth. For you have died and your life is hidden with Christ in God.

2 Corinthians 5:17

If any man be in Christ, he is a new creature; old things have passed away, behold, all things have become new.

When choosing God (Salvation), you are not choosing a fairytale, rose pedals, the easy road, and definitely not the quick road. Instead, you fully commit to a Mark 10:29-30 existence. With the understanding that choosing the Lord, and who and what He has for you, may not always manifest externally but the *eternal* Kingdom rewards are the primary focus. You build the now for where you are going.

Those who have accepted Christ will not be judged based on their sins but on their *works*. What we do with our time here on earth and whom we do it with is imperative for success. I believe that many people will unfortunately meet God on the day of judgment and see all the things they *could have* had, what they *could have* accomplished on earth and who they *could have* helped. However, fear, the desire to do things their way or in their time, and/or just due to a lack of commitment they negated the opportunity for them and those they were specifically called to on earth. You may be thinking, why does this matter if I made it to Heaven? Surely, I will no longer be concerned with what I did on earth. I implore you that commitment to Christ fully and His ways matter. Some things will not be done in this world because it is specifically for you to accomplish. Also, the greater the work, the greater reward; learn to build for where you are going to spend an eternity.

Be committed. Be committed to the process of becoming H.E.R. Heaven is birthing the Godly woman you are being molded into as soon as you accept Salvation. Your focus should be set on what is above i.e. what Heaven is saying about you and not what culture or what people generally on earth are saying about H.E.R. You are a new creation. Per verse three of Colossians, you have died and you are now hidden in Christ. When people *see* you now and your Kingdom committed new ways, they see Heaven en route through you. They see H.E.R.

DAY 6

TODAY'S AFFIRMATION

1. Father, I choose You. I trust your pathway. I am committed to Your plan.

2. I am committed to who and what You have for me. And in the *way* that it comes.

3. I fully recognize that my life may be written like those in Hebrews 11 who exited earth still hoping and believing in the unseen. Yet trusting that many would reap naturally and there was a greater reward eternally.

4. God, You chose me but today I choose You back, Your way, Your time, Your people and Your placement.

5. I fully commit to being the chosen of God and operating like it in my daily life.

6. I am committed to the God "chosen life" and pathway built for H.E.R.

WRITE YOUR OWN DAILY AFFIRMATION:

Day 7

"Painstaking Pathway"

Daniel 5:12; Daniel 6:3

Forasmuch as an excellent spirit, and knowledge, and understanding, interpreting of dreams, and shewing of hard sentences, and dissolving of doubts, were found in the same Daniel, whom the king named Belteshazzar: now let Daniel be called, and he will shew the interpretation. – **Daniel 5:12**

Then this Daniel was preferred above the presidents and princes, because an excellent spirit was in him; and the king thought to set him over the whole realm. **Daniel 6:3**

> Painstaking- done with or employing great care and thoroughness

Daniel is considered by many to have had an excellent spirit because of his discipline and dedication to God. Similarly, my hope is that you will dedicate your life to God by living under His disciplines through the spirit of excellence – spiritually, mentally, physically, and financially. In order to lead others, you have to advance the room in an area (at least one that they do not have). The area of progress may be expertise, unique talent, or solely the right that God chose you for it and no one else. God has chosen you to be committed to His plans via the *painstaking pathway*.

In this process, God will reveal, "who your people are" in order for you not to do it alone. The Lord will clearly pinpoint who is called to walk intimately with you amidst this critical time.

It is also important to note that there is no rush order on God's plan. From the biggest picture to the smallest minute detail, He has a plan. Those plans are best fulfilled through the Holy Spirit led Christ Believer. The business Christians handle is the business of God. All is done by His *timing*, His *way*, and His *order*. The "painstaking pathway" was/is His first order of business for Believers.

This pathway is not for the faint of heart, tradition strugglers (i.e. those who struggle with breaking from traditional paths), or those fearful about being wrong in the eyes of "others."

Exaltation comes from God and this is that time for you (if you are ready)!

DAY 7

TODAY'S AFFIRMATIONS:

1. I am equipped for this painstaking pathway. The hindrances, roadblocks or distractions the enemy or even my flesh would try to bring do not intimidate me as my eyes are focused on Jesus Christ.

2. I have an excellent spirit due to my intentional daily time with the Lord and my commitment to His *way*, His *timing* and His *order*. There is no resistance to God within me!

3. Because I am handling the Lord's plans with care, He will reveal to me all who are for me and together we will continually share His love and Salvation as we complete our assignments on the earth

4. I understand JESUS is the way, the truth and the life. There is no other way to the Father but by Him (John 14:6). As a result of me following the way of Christ, every good avenue is open to me.

5. I know that even if His way proves difficult at times, it is still the best way.

WRITE YOUR OWN DAILY AFFIRMATION:

Day 8

God is my Refuge...

PSALM 46:1

Refuge is the great escape from the troubled place. Refuge is a place of safety and peace. It is also a place where all of the non-disclosed matters of your life are sanctioned to rest. Jesus is our great escape, our refuge. He is our prepared place. When has the Lord ever disclosed one of your intimacies to another? If He did, he/she could be trusted with the information. Jesus now is preparing a place for us in heaven. A place filled with refuge to escape the vicissitudes of this world.

What I have discovered is people often know how to run to God as a place of refuge, but can He come to you? Synonyms to refuge are hiding place, sanctuary, and safety. The word tells us that His spirit is within us. Upon Salvation, we are reconciled with Christ. The Lord should be able to come…to live in you as a place of safety. Some people have an expectation that a particular person will be able to hold their weights or secrets of life. And never hear them repeated in the world again. But before you have that expectation for someone else, make sure you are that place for the One who has given you eternal life.

Characteristics of a refuge:

- Everyone does not have access (limited)
- What goes in does not go back out...*at least not in the same way* (protective over image)
- Peace, trust, solace reigns... it is a place of REST. To be strengthened to return for the next day or quest.

God is strength, so He does not need to be strengthened. However, can He trust you with the unknown? Can He disclose the secrets of others to you and you responsibly pray, cover and not disclose verbally or deliberately to another or mischaracterize him or her? Can you carry His peace and His presence? Are you unable to be a refuge or place of rest because you concern yourself or worry about matters He already has resolved?

Do you have reciprocal LOVE relationships? We cannot LOVE God, if we do not love our sisters and brothers (1 John 4:20).

Safe places in male relationships or female friendships have to be built. The requirements naturally differ for men as opposed to women. It boils down to *trust*. A sound person is not going to take rest in a place they do not feel safe. When being a refuge for a woman, trust and safety will often emulate consistency because this signifies protection. For women, you build by being consistent – doing what you say you are going to do and being who you say you are.

Men are not *generally* as verbal as women. Even in studying the development of boys as opposed to girls, tactile and motor skills are typically higher in male children. Verbal and linguistics are

DAY 8

increasingly higher for girls. If there are a lot of words, over sharing of men's proclivities and general faults be it with them (constant reminders of his wrongs) or others… trust will not be built. And refuge will not be taken.

Equally as important, I heard someone say once; men do not unpack secrets where they do not intend to stay. Additionally as it relates to men, you have to learn the art of "seasoning" your words.

Two Types of Seasoning

- -*Seasoning* relates to adding something *sweet* and the *right spice*. The delivery wins the gold. You have to know how to speak and deliver to that particular man. It does not mean that you are to be a pushover. But it is given with love (1 Cor. 13) and always based in truth. Remember to add seasoning, in this regard what worked for one may not work for all. Learn the right ingredients for that particular man.
- -"**Season**ing." Some things are best delivered in the correct season. You have to learn to season your release of certain conversations. Everything is not to be disclosed in winter i.e. an extremely down day or time. Discipline and self-control with the tongue will aid in this area. The majority of words for men should be left in prayer. Prayer should never be underestimated. It is where the Lord works on hearts and gives schema on how we as women can be a safe refuge. Therefore, when it is time to talk, you become a secure and a God-sanctioned environment.

Women are naturally a refuge for others, as we are instinctively nurturers, we have natural wombs and are seed carriers. Wise women know how to be a refuge to others in a way that the Lord needs us to be.

The wise woman recognizes how to not only take refuge in Jesus but to return the same. This is a level of maturation that comes with walking and seeking the Lord intimately.

DAY 8

TODAY'S AFFIRMATION:

1. Thank You Father for being my "great escape." I have learned how to not solely be a receiver but I am now dedicated to being a trusted place for You.

2. This reciprocal relationship we have of refuge now is the soliloquy of You for me and I for You. It has seeped into my treatment of all men.

3. As a woman, I know how to be a refuge for those that are entrusted to me by You. Be it my husband, relationships generally, ministry, family or friends.

4. I am a place of rest because *I am rested*.

5. My God has everything that concerns me. I will have and see everything that He has said, even if it is through the eyes and hands of what I birth.

6. I believe and trust God forevermore. He is incapable of being or doing anything less than the truth!

WRITE YOUR OWN DAILY AFFIRMATION:

Day 9

"I am beyond a flower; I am a garden"

Isaiah 58:11

The Lord will guide you continually, and satisfy your soul in drought, and strengthen your bones; you shall be like a well-watered garden, *and like a spring of water, whose waters do not fail.*

This verse is discussing a famine, drought or some form of devastation in the land that has caused a deficit of water. However, despite the conditions in the land, the scripture says you will be a well in a dry land. Taking this symbolically, you can be a wealth resource when everyone else is experiencing paucity. You can be a spring of wellness for those who are sick. An oasis amidst an ocean or literal place of escape for someone. Culturally, water often represents life. You can be a source of life in a place that is viewed or feels like death.

Matriculation from a flower to a "well-watered" garden is not when you give your flower away. Instead, it is when you produce multiple flowers until there is a garden that surrounds you. To note, gardens are not produced without enduring seasons of variant weather, the removal or killing of what attempts to kill what is making you grow, and that curse word for some, TIME.

Women are natural producers. Women have the capability of turning dry land into an oasis, a drought into a wetland, we pronounce life to what is dead, we provide healing to what is not well and famines never scare us because we have the inherent ability to produce food. We are producers.

The woman who has graduated from a flower to a full garden has groomed others to be like or better than her. She freely gives because there are multiple seeds inside her that will continue to produce. She also understands that the symbolism above covers every area spiritually, mentally, emotionally, and physically.

DAY 9

TODAY'S AFFIRMATION:

1. God has created me as a place of escape. I am an oasis to every ocean.

2. I am a spring of life that provides hope that all will be well because I carry the spring of wellness inside of me.

3. The Lord has watered me so well; I am springing forth an entire garden that physically exudes beauty and provides an eternal well to all who may be lost.

4. As a woman, I fully embrace the natural maturation process of time, growth, and production.

5. I am a producer. I serve as a resource of life and wellness for all that I am called to. All people and things naturally grow and produce when connected to me.

6. Today, I am not a sole flower but a well-watered garden.

WRITE YOUR OWN DAILY AFFIRMATION:

Day 10

GrOw is divinely connected to "GO"

1 Peter 2:2

Like newborn babies, crave pure spiritual milk, so that by it you may grow up in your salvation,

As I help others navigate through the details and plans of God, I noticed that we often try to make it make sense. If A, then B. If I want a home, I need this amount of financial increase. I have found that all you need is the divine "GO" from God. Once He gives permission for you to embark upon the next step, all the other things will not matter and He will provide along the way. Also, as you go, you will grow. It is inevitable. I have been mandated to not only GO, but to also GROW in this season. And my mandated GO is on acceleration.

Sometimes you have to go in order to grow.

TODAY'S AFFIRMATION

1. I am determined to grow in this season. Stagnation, fear, people nor I will hold me back.
2. I understand my "growing" is divinely connected to my "going".
3. Today, I am moving on whatever God says without deliberation or debate. Here I GrOw again!
4. As I go, my growth is being accelerated.

DAY 10

WRITE YOUR OWN DAILY AFFIRMATION:

Day 11

"Consider thy ways"

Haggai 1:5-7

Now this is what the LORD Almighty says: "Give careful thought to your ways. You have planted much, but harvested little. You eat, but never have enough. You drink, but never have your fill. You put on clothes, but are not warm. You earn wages, only to put them in a purse with holes in it." This is what the LORD Almighty says: "Give careful thought to your ways.

I had to consider my ways this morning. I received loads of revelation and knowledge on cycles, specifically the discontinuance of the wrong ones. God furthered that obedience to Him unlocks the door to provision; thusly, permanently eliminating ways that led to erroneous cycles.

Provision- the act of supplying
Synonym: giving, delivering

We all need the Lord's provision in one area or another. The key to the supply room is doing what He says. Do not use the other key of "trying to figure it all out" because it will only frustrate your purpose.

Daily, we have to consider our ways. Is obedience to God immediate? If immediate results are desired in situations, it is wise to reflect on what is being done, and consider thy ways. Decree and declare daily~ I have clarity in my mind. I follow God's gateway for my provision and no lack exists within me.

If there is any lack of provision in any area of your life – consider thy ways.

We have to trust that we serve the God of the Holy Bible and His provision is directly related to our obedience. However, His provision may come in a way not expected. So, we have to turn off the mental deliberation. We have to turn off the poverty mindset. And turn on the trust; learn to rest in pure obedience to God.

In this place, we will find not only the provision of God but also the abundance of His provision.

DAY 11

TODAY'S AFFIRMATIONS:

1. God's gateway of provision surrounds and follows me.
2. I have clarity in my mind. Confusion is not a part of me.
3. I walk in the overflow of God due to my obedience to Him and lack can never hold me.
4. I live, think, and move in abundance.
5. God's wealth is attracted to me.
6. I serve the God of unlimited resources and no need does He withhold from His own. I have all that is needed and God has provided.
7. Because I ensure my ways are in alignment with the Lord's ways, all negative cycles are broken today!!!

WRITE YOUR OWN DAILY AFFIRMATION:

Day 12

"God's communication is love letters to me"

John 10:27

My sheep listen to my voice; I know them, and they follow me.

I speak praises and adorations to the only true and living God, the Father of Jesus Christ and the precious Holy Ghost this day because You alone are worthy! The Trinity is wholeness – completeness – exactness – and most importantly *love*. Thank You for Your love, for who You are. Your love purges my very nature of everything unlike You – Your love is healing. Thank You for healing me.

Today, I am equipped for all that life or the day may bring because of Your love. You have taught me that the voice of God is small and still. As I purposely still myself before the great I am in this moment, I yearn and thank You in advance for Your communication to me. Teach me Your voice so I will never follow any strange voices. Help me to never love my voice or the voice of others more than Yours. Father, help me to understand that Your silence actually speaks and Your presence does more than one-word release from me to You.

It is an honor and a privilege to hear Your communication with me. Every word, breath, correction, dream, warning, prophecy, even Your silence; God inspired song, book or poem are love letters to me.

Thank You that the grace and grant of Your voice is love!

DAY 12

TODAY'S AFFIRMATIONS:

1. I am honored by the grant of Your voice that spoke what is seen and unseen.
2. Thank You Lord for teaching me to honor Your words in whatever form they come, it is a privilege to hear.
3. Your communication is love letters to me.
4. Father, Your presence is healing.
5. Thank You Lord that You will never leave nor forsake me.

WRITE YOUR OWN DAILY AFFIRMATION:

Day 13

"Accountability as the link from start to finish"

Ecclesiastes 9:11

I have seen something else under the sun: The race is not to the swift or the battle to the strong, nor does food come to the wise or wealth to the brilliant or favor to the learned; but time and chance happen to them all.

When people struggle to start it is often due to all the "what if's" or "it's not my time" scenarios. However, the best way to get something started is simply to begin. Drop every excuse and just do it. Society can over-intellectualize a matter until decades or sadly a lifetime has passed, just do it! No excuses. In my sorority, we often say that excuses are the tools of the incompetent, those wishing to utilize the use of such tools are seldom better than anything other than excuses.

Starting something is not normally a problem for people but the element of completion often is. Finishes do not happen alone. The Body of Christ is meant to function as a whole body. Unfortunately, in the Spirit, we often appear disjointed because so many of us are attempting to have completion by operating solo. There are parts of this life process that require you to walk alone (even if you are without man for a season, you are never without God). However, in most things, we are meant to spur one another on to the finish line. In races, there are people that are *fellow runners*, the crowd for *cheering* and the coaches who *aid you* in the process. All of these participants are necessary for your completion. Ensure your team has those who run with you, cheer you on, and aid you generally to finish.

Before you complete, divine insight will be in your path from a settled one or ones. Someone that has completed where you are and he or she will give insight to steer you on the perfect road to completion. In this context, accountability matters. When mentor and mentee relationships are studied from a Biblical context, the mentee typically sought after the one with greater experience and knowledge in order to glean. Put pride, fear and anything else aside that would hinder you from completion. Find and glean from the individual or individuals that you can hold yourself accountable to in order to finish your race! Note these people may be what you consider as an unlikely source, like significantly younger. God uses whom He desires. Remember Christ lived only 33 years and many followers of His ministry spanned all ages including those who were significantly older than Him. Accountability serves as the divine link from start to finish.

The race is not given to the swift, but to the one that endures to the end.

As you consider finishing, understand the significance of finishing well. Some people finish but they do not complete the race well. Pace yourself, get the insight, take in and learn all that is necessary in your process in order to ensure a healthy finish. All of these elements aid in a "full" finish.

Lastly, the actual "finishing" should be coupled with a celebration time. This is important because these moments are not always fully felt or embraced. As you finish, recognize that you have worked hard. Therefore, it is time to take it all in. "This" race is complete.

* * *

Take a moment and write down everything you have finished in life. I mean everything…1st grade, a calendar day, an article, an unhealthy relationship. Put it on the wall as a reminder that completion is in you and today you have the divine insight to do it better than before.

TODAY'S AFFIRMATIONS:

1. Although I may walk alone, I will never be lonely.
2. Today, I will begin the journey to complete a necessary heart goal.
3. Incompetency is not becoming of me nor excuses a part of my communication.
4. I recognize I do not have to finish by myself and I seek after God-ordained, qualified ones to guide me to the finish line.
5. I am pacing myself in this race of life with the understanding that I am in competition with no man. My life race is solely my own.
6. I celebrate every finish as a win because I understand the fight and effort it took to complete it.

DAY 13

WRITE YOUR OWN DAILY AFFIRMATION:

Day 14

"TRUST"

Romans 10:11 NLT

As the Scriptures tell us, "Anyone who trusts in him will never be disgraced."

Trusting in the Lord is the first way to build trust in other relationships. Our ways and thoughts are generally not like God's until we submit them to Him. Therefore, the best way to trust in God is through practice. Allow the word of the Lord in Romans 10:11 to remind you that anyone who trusts in God will never be disgraced.

How do you trust Him?

Trust in God is spurred by intimacy and maintained in Faith. You trust in the Lord by building a relationship with Him. Talk to Him, spend your time with Him, serve Him, worship Him and the relationship will develop in the process. As time proceeds, you will begin to learn the character of God through intimacy. Pray daily that your Faith will not fail during moments of adversity. Trusting in God is a choice and belief that He can and will do all that He has promised. You do not have to do anything extra, simply obey and rest.

"Into me I see" aka *Intimacy*...learn how to be a trusted one

We live in a society where many things are on display for the world to see and privacy is not honored. For instance, marital bedroom acts being in conversation beyond the spouses.

The media does not honor or respect the privacy of families during difficult moments and seemingly every milestone has to be documented by a social media post. Shouting or sharing an intimate event does not make it more or less true.

As wise women, we must realize that the evidence of deep intimacy shall bear fruit. What does intimacy have to do with trust? Intimacy is a vulnerable place, you are seeing into a person's inward man that holds vulnerabilities, privacy and the untold. A person of wisdom is not likely to be deeply intimate with someone they cannot trust to hold the truth of who he or she is. When you find people who have trust issues, there has likely been a violation of intimacy. A sexual violation, secrets divulged, judgment of an insecure place and/or over-sharing of privacies has occurred. This is an elementary concept but the judger; a person who cannot hold privacies or loud talker is not typically the one who people trust. Proverbs 16:28 states that a whisperer separates close friends. On a different level, I reiterate the question, can God trust you with His heart? Or does everything He shares proceed from your mouth void of care or concern of its impact on others? This is not about keeping secrets but people must learn the art of privacy.

Some things that are exposed during intimacy are just for the intimate ones and solitude in knowing that what is to be shared will "produce" in due season.

DAY 14

As you develop intimacy with the Father, remember everything spoken during times of intimacy should not be repeated, seen, heard, smelt, felt or known. Some moments should be left solely for God and you or your loved one and you to savor. The savoring of intimacy promotes growth that ultimately becomes visible to all. For instance, have you ever noticed a pregnant woman has a distinct look?

Typically, her hair and nails will grow, her skin will glow and as the seed of intimacy continues, her belly will grow. The mother will not have to say, "I am pregnant," her intimate seed will be evident via production. When a person has spent significant time with God and truly knows Him, there is a mark of beauty, a certain glow that he or she carries. There are many things that are formed during our intimate time with the Lord that may include fruits of the Spirit, Godly wisdom, peace, love inward positive change or direction are all signs that you have been intimate with the Lord.

Choose to trust not control

Once you choose to trust in God and God can trust in you, life changes. Your perspective shifts for life and relationships alter for the better. True trust in God, relinquishes your control and you completely rest in His way.

TODAY'S AFFIRMATIONS:

1. I trust God and equally important, God can trust me. I am trustworthy.

2. I value and consider it a great honor for those who allow me to hold their intimacies that I protect with a guard over my lips and heart.

3. I am a holder of privacies without judgment and I relinquish all weights only to God.

DAY 14

WRITE YOUR OWN DAILY AFFIRMATION:

Day 15

SPEAK
Open your mouth

Psalms 81:10

"…Open your mouth wide and I will fill it."

OPEN YOUR MOUTH. The mouths of women have been muzzled in so many ways generationally, corporately, politically, and in some settings spiritually. This is an agenda not birthed from Heaven. Women's words are eternal wells for the lives of others and resting places for many.

It is important to note, women who give life-giving words are filled with life and that filling comes from the Lord. We have to seek Christ intimately so He can fill our mouths and give us what to say. On the contrary, there are women who are not filled with His Spirit and the fruit of their words and actions are evidence of this fact. Proverbs mentions many times about a nagging or quarrelsome woman and how it is reminiscent of a dripping faucet or it is better to be on a roof than with this type of woman (Proverbs 21:9, Proverbs 21:19, and Proverbs 27:15).

Today, make a decision to be filled only with the words of the Lord. I believe that if you open your mouth and speak only what God says, only words of life, words of purpose and Holy correction, this world will change for the better. The Proverbs 31 woman is a mother speaking to her son, a future King about the type of woman to choose, a loving mother's words is always a source of encouragement and gives latitude for growth. Women are life-givers intrinsically; therefore, our output (if done correctly) gives life.

A woman's words can call forth Kings and Queens with a single affirmation, give credence to ensure generations are protected against enemies (Esther) or serve as vile manipulation that severs power and all hope for tomorrow (Delilah).

Be mindful of what you release and to whom you are releasing it. Generationally, spiritually and naturally, a woman's words have the power of life or death; so, choose life (Proverbs 18:21)

Today, speak what God says, render truths, *open your mouth* wide and *speak* life!

DAY 15

TODAY'S AFFIRMATION

1. I speak only what God sanctions me to release.
2. I am a life-giver.
3. Everything that I speak to is commanded to live and grows.
4. All my releases are birthed by the truth of the Lord.
5. Men, women, boys, and girls from all walks enjoy the breath of my presence because they know I carry the air that releases them to grow.
6. Today, I OPEN MY MOUTH WIDE and intentionally with the expectation of the Lord filling what I speak with LIFE.

WRITE YOUR OWN DAILY AFFIRMATION:

Day 16

"Healing hands, Healing hugs, and Healing conversations"

1 Corinthians 12:27

Now you are the body of Christ, and each one of you is a part of it.

I thank God that today You have given me healing hands, healing hugs and healing conversations. We (the Body of Christ) are to be the hands and feet of Christ as we embody His Holy Spirit. Today, do not wait for opportunities of ministry to reach out to you via a visit or a call. You are the church! Everyday that you are given, take the autonomous steps to provide the healing power of Jesus Christ via your hands, hugs and especially your conversations.

This journal is laced with the power of touch and words because women naturally have a nurturing disposition verbally that can also be felt. Some women have to practice the way to exude all of these things, but it is there – resident within. Use the healing virtue that the Lord has placed inside of you as a woman and share it today via your hands, hugs and conversation. Take some time to listen, give of your time and space. Practice makes perfect.

TODAY'S AFFIRMATIONS:

1. My words have life.
2. My hands and hugs bring divine healing through my love.
3. I have accepted the set daily mission to be the hands and feet of Christ.
4. My healing hands, healing hugs, and healing conversations are and will be responsible for bringing countless souls to the Kingdom. It will also nurture other believers to reach their full potential in God.
5. As a woman, I innately have the power to nurture verbally in such a powerful way it can be felt.

WRITE YOUR OWN DAILY AFFIRMATION:

Day 17

"The God id of she/ her/ hers"
Femininity in the eyes of God

Genesis 2:18-25

The LORD God said, "It is not good for the man to be alone. I will make a helper suitable for him." Now the LORD God had formed out of the ground all the wild animals and all the birds in the sky. He brought them to the man to see what he would name them; and whatever the man called each living creature, that was its name. So the man gave names to all the livestock, the birds in the sky and all the wild animals. But for Adam no suitable helper was found. So the LORD God caused the man to fall into a deep sleep; and while he was sleeping, he took one of the man's ribs and then closed up the place with flesh. Then the LORD God made a woman from the rib he had taken out of the man, and he brought her to the man. The man said, "This is now bone of my bones and flesh of my flesh; she shall be called 'woman,' for she was taken out of man." That is why a man leaves his father and mother and is united to his wife, and they become one flesh. Adam and his wife were both naked, and they felt no shame.

> Femininity is defined as qualities or attributes
> regarded as characteristics of women.

Feminine qualities vary by region, culture, and era. Some women of today's *era* believe in the power of choice and there is an array of feminine *cultural* styles. The current dominant cohort's group's (Millennials) mothers may identify more with the television mom Claire Huxtable while this generation's mother's woman (Baby Boomers) id was similar to the show "Leave it to Beaver" era. Africa culturally is known to hold their matriarchs in high esteem. While in many Indian cultures, the women are often barely seen and rarely heard (publicly). In hospitals, pink is still for girls.

All of these feminine ideals are made and people-influenced. These things do not make you a woman.

Family traits, cultural feminine characteristics, the size of your hips, length of your lashes, complexion, bra size, nail color, nor hairstyles make you a woman. Femininity by God is innate…pre-chosen by God. It is who you are. Your femininity is settled in Heaven. Godly femininity is who you are created to be. However, there is wisdom in the embrace of some of the aforementioned in balance. For instance, it is not healthy to present your femininity in the wrong way. Too much cleavage or a lack of moderation in your dress is not a part of God's femininity. Nor is concealing your curves completely or natural woman God givens in order to hide that you are a female.

* * *

In my rearing, femininity exuded great hygiene, feminine clothes, long hair, pearls, well groomed, and beauty to name some. There is absolutely nothing wrong with a culture or family adapting a certain idea of femininity.

DAY 17

> Except this…as Christians we are not adapters. We are defined as by who God says we are.

A woman's femininity is especially God produced. You may like basketball and shorts over heels and tea. Preferring one of the aforementioned over the other does not make you more or less of a woman. In Genesis or the infamously quoted Proverbs 31, there is not an emphasis on how the woman looks. Instead, character, work ethic, helping others, serving family, being multifaceted and what she produced depicts the Godly woman. We are done with semantics as the true essence of a woman. Being a woman and Godly femininity is inborn.

I am she/her/hers

She/ her / hers is the current cultural label that you desire to be identified as a woman and these specific pronouns are the way you request to be addressed. This usage is popular in many corporate settings.

The issue that I have found with the current trend of culturally defined femininity is that it steers away from the Biblical definition and often emasculates men in order to seemingly empower the woman. Also, there is more of a focus on the external qualities of women. As believing women, the original Creator should solely shape our identity and feminine existence. What God says about woman is all the true empowerment we need to live on purpose.

Who does God say woman is?

To truly understand a name, you have to view the origin. Biblically, what is the origin and design of a woman?

Genesis 2:18-25
Defining H.E.R. by God

God creates H.E.R.
The woman was created to help (fills voids; *not helpless*).
Women can do what men cannot (biologically)
i.e. produce and multiply.
We make things whole. A sperm alone is
a seed but in a woman it is life.
A true woman is found in *Eden* (a place of rest and wellness).

She/her/hers is the woman of the original Eden. Pristine, abundant and natural beauty describes her. She is a place of consistent rest.

A person may enter only with divine permission. Her love is for all and it is healing for all souls who accept her.

When you find or experience a woman of true femininity, she is found in a place of Eden.

What is Eden?
A. Paradise
B. An eternal garden
C. Constant place of rest
D. Pristine
E. Abundant natural beauty

When you see these traits, you have not just encountered a
woman (biologically) but one who is Godly feminine.

There is nothing wrong generally speaking if you have adopted the qualities of your family, culture and "some" society traits that are quoted as feminine. However, true femininity must come from the Creator. If you desire God's true traits for femininity, you have to

DAY 17

first know them and secondly embrace them in order for it to exude. For some women, this may be harder than for others. Violations, words, experiences, the coarseness of the course of life, rapes, misrepresentation of what a woman is or simply not knowing (prior to today) what true Godly femininity is and what your Creator says about the design of who you are. Well, now you know. Also, God will continue to help you! He will heal you if necessary and it begins with today's confession for H.E.R listed below.

Please note I did not name "people" or relationships being a contributing factor of reasons true Godly femininity may not have been embraced. Always, remember to direct healing at the root as opposed to the individual. You will heal faster this way.

TODAY'S AFFIRMATIONS:

1. I am she/her/hers as God has designed me.

2. I am a true woman of God that can only be found in a place of Eden. Everyone that is allowed to enter the world of who I am will have rest no matter how deep their prior pain.

3. I am a well-watered garden (Eden) that mandates increase. Everything I command with my mouth does not die but multiply!

4. I am perfectly "molded and shaped" by God. I embrace every shape, color, curve and strand of this life season. I am beautifully and wonderfully made. My idiosyncrasies were God's forethought that separates and affirms the uniqueness He stamped me with.

5. Every man to whom I am assigned (family, friend, ministry or professionally) will have an intrinsic pleasure and an emboldened voice and declarative stature from my presence, aroma and look alone.

6. My past choices, experiences or erroneous views or ways do not altar the essence of the woman and femininity I was created to walk in.

7. The man for which God created for me, we operate as one and revel in our nakedness (truths).

8. I am naturally beautiful and pristine. I'm a generation's birther, designed well and intentionally by God.

I hope this helps she/ her / hers embrace H.E.R. Godly femininity.

DAY 17

WRITE YOUR OWN DAILY AFFIRMATION:

Day 18

"Setting Place"

Romans 12:2

Do not conform to the pattern of this world, but be transformed by the renewing of your mind. Then you will be able to test and approve what God's will is-his good, pleasing and perfect will.

You have to become a settled place. Something or someone that is "settled" is synonymous with sure. Without waver… consistent. *The go to*. How is a settled place created? It begins with your mind. God wants us to be His settling place by renewing our minds. There are many things today that would attempt to attack and then attach to your mind. The news, oftentimes workplaces or families can be filled with scenarios that would attempt to dismantle your mind and disarm what you know to be true according to the word of God. Romans 12:2 reminds us that we are in this world and not of it, daily we have to strive to renew our minds. Renewal occurs best by settling in the One who has been consistent since He created time i.e. the Lord. As you press into the place of His presence consistently, you will in turn adapt the same characteristics.

Be His consistent place. A settling place for the Holy Ghost is created through a consecrated lifestyle. Ask God to help you to be just that and heal any place within that would disrupt it. Invite His divine mighty power through prayer to create a mind that is consistent with His nature and ways.

Peace is a created avenue for you. As you make room and make a settling place for God beginning in your mind. He will inwardly dine with you and allow peace to be imparted.

When you have Godly peace, purpose is often birthed, creativity thrives and movement works in the sequence of God's plan.

Holiness, sacredness and sanctity are the perquisites to operating consistently in a settled place.

Have you ever found yourself to be all over the place mentally, spiritually, emotionally or even naturally? It is likely due to the need for mind renewal by way of consecration in order for you to receive the impartation of God's peace. In moments where you feel unsettled, wait on the Lord and you shall renew your strength (Isaiah 40:31).

Be the Lord's setting place. He does not say He will always speak, He said He will never leave nor forsake you. It is about God's presence. Where His presence is, there is fullness of joy, liberty and all that is needed.

If the setting of your mind or environment becomes contaminated due to the allowance of life's vicissitude's to infiltrate and stay, the place has to be cleared again. As a point of emphasis, it is best to live in a place of consecration to avoid your mind becoming unsettled. Consecration is filled with all things God, such as daily prayer, love, Christian fellowship, self-care, consistently reading and studying the word of God. Live your life daily in a freed place of renewal and you will not only be a settled place for God, for others, but also yourself.

DAY 18

TODAY'S AFFIRMATIONS:

1. I created a settled place within by living a consecrated life for God and my mind is constantly renewed.

2. I am certain of who God is and I trust the work He is creating within me.

3. Consistency with and intimacy in the presence of the Lord breaks the barriers of all things against me.

4. Although I am in this world, I am not of it. My mind, body and soul belong to Jesus Christ.

5. If no one else is willing, I am determined to serve God. I am His trusted settled place.

6. I am here God. Your servant is listening.

7. All my paths are straight because I am a settled place.

WRITE YOUR OWN DAILY AFFIRMATION:

Day 19

Just A.S.K. HIM

Matthew 7:7-8

"Ask and it will be given to you; seek and you will find; knock and the door will be opened to you. For everyone who asks receives; the one who seeks finds; and to the one who knocks, the door will be opened.

Let's deal with Daddy issues

~Who is your daddy?

Many women are dealing with issues because they do not know their daddy. I am not speaking of your biological dad but your spiritual Father, the creator of the heavens and earth.

Your daddy is God, the one who loves you so dearly that He sent His only begotten son (Jesus Christ) to die and rise for your sins. I am taking my time to explain that not only do you have a daddy but also He LOVES you so deeply that He sacrificed His only son's life in order for you to live (eternally). However, He is a great Father and gives excellent gifts (Matthew 7:11); your Father also desires for you to have great things on this earth. Stability, purpose, successful plans, answers to questions, peace and love.

This journal would be remiss and pointless for many if you do not know Christ. Today is a great day (if you have not already) to accept the gift of Salvation. Jesus Christ died so that we may have eternal life upon His return. First, repent aloud of every sin committed known and unknown.

Next, if you confess aloud that Jesus Christ is Lord and believe in your heart that Jesus died and rose again for your sins (Romans 10:9-10), then today, you are saved! Welcome to the Kingdom of God.

Your acceptance of Salvation is the key to eternal life and avoidance of eternal damnation. Salvation does not necessarily eliminate daddy issues. Some people project absentee dad issues, abuse, and the desire for more time or an entirely different dad in general onto God. Others simply do not know Him well enough to truly embody the relationship He has designed for His children fully.

How do you obtain these things? Just a.s.k. Him.

Ask, and it will be given to you; seek, *and you will find;* knock, *and the door will be opened to you. For everyone who asks receives, and he who seeks finds, and to him who knocks it will be opened* (Matthew 7:7-8).

You have to keep on asking, seeking and knocking and He will respond. Do not allow past experiences, erroneous past findings or weariness to misguide you in your relationship with your daddy. God wants you to win!

DAY 19

TODAY'S AFFIRMATIONS:

1. Persistence is the gateway to the door of unlimited opportunities (quote from *Pure Serenity Counseling*).
2. I persistently a.s.k. God in all things with my daily pursuit of God.
3. I confess daily Jesus Christ is Lord.
4. I denounce any and all word curses spoken by me, on me, on the generation or on my bloodline. My mind, body, soul and Spirit belong to the only true and living God.
5. No matter what has or has not occurred in my life, I know God wants me to win!

WRITE YOUR OWN DAILY AFFIRMATION:

Day 20

Masked Sender

2 Thessalonians 2:1-3

Concerning the coming of our LORD Jesus Christ and our being gathered to him, we ask you, brothers and sisters, not to become easily unsettled or alarmed by the teaching allegedly from us-whether by a prophecy or by word of mouth or by letter-asserting that the day of the LORD has already come. Don't let anyone deceive you in any way, for that day will not come until the rebellion occurs and the man of lawlessness is revealed, the man doomed to destruction.

~ Learn to focus in order to avoid the *masked sender*…

There are many things and people masking as the truth. 2 Thessalonians 2:3 speaks of the time before Christ's return, there will be a great falling away. Falling away in the scriptures is ascribed to people being greatly deceived. There is only one way to prevent deception and to stay out of the falling away remnant, and that is keeping your focus on God. When you are so intertwined with His presence, what He is saying and what He has for you to do, you will not fall into the trap of listening to strange voices.

A while ago, I had a dream where a familiar person gave me a great financial proposal that I immediately trusted because of our relationship. Upon my acceptance of the financial proposition, the enemy immediately took root in my finances but not in the way one would think. My money immediately grew, I was able to pay off debt, sow into businesses and have a significant consistent side income at least for a moment. However, the Lord showed me spiritually that my dependency and trust was in the money as opposed to the route He had for me.

Although, the Lord showed me that I did have financial success, He also revealed that He would not allow the influence He had planned for me because the source was not Him. It reminded me of Gideon when he had to decrease the troops so they would not try to take the feat as their strength as opposed to giving honor to God for allowing their success (Judges 7). God showed me His financial plan was for me to create income in only the way He instructed. No, I did not know the duration of how long the commas in my account would take. Yes, it would be a process and not an overnight success story but when the endurance testimony is shared, people would identify with the struggle of the process, and the Lord keeping me. Anything other than this pathway was not the plan of Christ for my life.

The Lord warned me further to be careful of the masked sender. Masked senders pose themselves as truth and in reality they are only there to get you off the pathway of God. Family, friends and some of your favorite relationships can be used knowingly or unknowingly in this way. To avoid this pitfall, stay focused on God. Know and commit to the way He has stated your path should go. Therefore, any contrary suggestion, you will quickly identify as the masked sender and abort that suggested plan.

DAY 20

TODAY'S AFFIRMATION

John 10:4-5

1. I am equipped to know the voice of God.
2. I am the sheep of the Lord.
3. I am not a follower of strange voices.
4. I am focused on God.
5. The spirit of suggestion that speaks contrary to Christ, I immediately identify as the masked sender, and do not accept the proposal.

WRITE YOUR OWN DAILY AFFIRMATION:

Day 21

You've got GAINS!

1 Timothy 6:6 (NLT)

Yet true godliness with contentment is itself great wealth.

You've got gains! I wish you would see yourself and your situations in the spiritual eyes of the Lord. The Father is ever moving, never sleeping, and always-working on your behalf. As a result, you are making "gains" that have not yet materialized naturally.

As you ascertain yourself via a relationship with God, His nature will become yours (Godliness). Be sure to couple this state of existence with being content. The Spiritual always precedes the natural. This means God will first send a command and/or download a future promise spiritually. However, it may be a moment before it manifests itself naturally. Therefore, bask in your spiritual gains, be content in all He has shown you to come and feel the great wealth of trusting in God.

TODAY'S AFFIRMATION

1. I am content in my trust in the Lord.
2. The Lord is leading my life.
3. My wealth is not limited to what is seen (natural) but I also have great wealth in what is not seen (spiritual).
4. My mind, will, and emotions pursue the Lord relentlessly; therefore, I have natural and eternal gains!

DAY 21

WRITE YOUR OWN DAILY AFFIRMATION:

Day 22

Be willing to be last.

Matthew 20:16

The last will be first and the first will be last.

The reality is we are all on different timetables and that is completely satisfactory. It may take you longer to get where you are going, but the goal is to finish. *Be willing to be last* if that means that you will actually have completion. There are so many people that reroute or quit before the procurement of a deeply desired goal due to their unwillingness to be last. These individuals have let people rush them to a state of nothingness or living underneath their destiny. The word is clear that the last shall be first and the first will be last. There are heavenly rewards for those who endure to the end and win.

Be willing to be last. This is not something that is taught but it should be. Success in some ways can be defined as the termination of attempts before achieving the desired outcome. The word attempt in the definition is plural. Therefore, sometimes before you have success in what you are attempting to attain, you may have to make repeated attempts before obtaining success. We live in a seemingly instantaneous society that promotes everything being actualized in certain time frames in order to be successful.

For instance, there are views that it is necessary to finish school by this date or season in life, marry at a particular age, have children by a certain time, buy a home in a specific season of life, have a cemented career, and decent salary before 40 are all loudly spoken cultural norms. But occasionally God will require you to stand at the end of the line and maintain a Godly character in the process. For His sake especially, be willing to be last.

Finally, even if you do have areas where you are the first, be sure that you are not the only; leave the door open for others to come behind you.

DAY 22

TODAY'S AFFIRMATIONS:

1. I recognize that success in some areas requires multiple attempts. I will persevere and not terminate my attempts until I win!
2. Even if I am last, I know my reward will be great.
3. Success is redefined by whenever I finish.
4. I am willing to be last if that means that I am a finisher.
5. In every area that I am a finisher, I will work hard to maintain Godly character as an example for others.

WRITE YOUR OWN DAILY AFFIRMATION:

Day 23

Do not discount spiritual seeds

~ Hosea 10:12 NLT

I said, 'Plant the good seeds of righteousness, and you will harvest a crop of love. *Plow up the hard ground of your hearts,* for now is the time to seek the *Lord, that he may come* and shower righteousness upon you.'

"Do not discount spiritual seeds." I recall this journal moment so clearly when I heard the voice of the Lord speak those words to me. I was not in the best place emotionally and was erroneously recounting different scenarios. I was telling the Father where I desired to be in my career and financially. He asked me in return what I considered as my greatest accomplishment. My response sincerely was and still is my relationship with God is my greatest success. For a long time, this was a place of embarrassment. I felt there should be something more I should be doing. I did not realize how much I was being defined by temporal roles and titles as my leverage stamp in society…until the Lord explained further.

Spiritual seeds are those things we do solely for God without the thought of a return. For example, the daily maintenance of our relationship with Him (reading and studying the Word of God, prayer, and worship); doing things for others in need that may be classified as spiritual or natural, loving and being kind generally. All of these that I have described may be classified as spiritual seeds. God explained that what is done for Him should not be discounted as nothing; He will surely cause you to have a reward on this earth and even more in the life to come.

As a result, do not discount all of the great spiritual seeds you sow daily, you will receive your just reward!

TODAY'S AFFIRMATION

1. I am not discounting the spiritual work that occurs daily in my life.
2. I am not defined by temporal positions or titles.
3. God is the only leverage stamp needed for my life.
4. I am shifting my perspective regarding success. My goal is to make my greatest success my relationship with Jesus Christ.
5. I am intentionally sowing daily into the eternal place.

WRITE YOUR OWN DAILY AFFIRMATION:

Day 24

"Give it a name"

Luke 8:29-30

For He had commanded the unclean spirit to come out of the man. For it had often seized him, and he was kept under guard, bound with chains and shackles; and he broke the bonds and was driven by the demon into the wilderness. Jesus asked him, saying, "What is your name?" And he said, "Legion" because many demons had entered him.

There are certain things we have to deal with by name. Names have power because they provide meaning and serve as identifiers. When babies are born or things are birthed generally, it is given a name or some type of classification or identification. Even in seeking deliverance from anything not of God, it is often wise to get the name so you know the origin.

Do you have some things that you desire to part with? Give it a name. Birthing, deliverance or freedom will not come from which you are unable to say or solely do not want to name.

TODAY'S AFFIRMATIONS:

Today, I name aloud every hindrance:

_____ you must leave my life now.

_____ you must leave my life now.

_____ you must leave my life now.

_____ you must leave my life now.

I decree and declare that the blood of Jesus covers me and I walk in wholeness and victory over every area.

DAY 24

WRITE YOUR OWN DAILY AFFIRMATION:

Day 25

The When/Win Situation

"Never dim your light even if it is blinding to others"
Adversity track

John 1:4-9

In Him was life, and the life was the light of men. And the light shines in the darkness, and the darkness did not [a]comprehend it.

There was a man sent from God, whose name was John. *This man came for a witness, to bear witness of the Light, that all through him might believe. He was not that Light, but was sent* to bear witness of *that Light. That*[b] was the true Light which gives light to every man coming into the world.

Understand that your when is divinely connected to your win. On the adversity track, all dimming or blocks are not necessarily from people. The Lord intentionally sets some blocks. However, when He shines the light on you or whispers, "now is the time." Your *when* has officially shifted into a *winning* season.

Adversities will come but the end of that track is the light of your win. The woes of life coupled with naysayers would advocate for you not to shine when this triumphant day occurs. Do not listen! Never dim your light even if it is blinding to others. Your light will be either a drawing for those who desire a closer walk with Christ or a dissenter for others who are resisting the pull of the Lord.

You were created to not only win but to shine!!!

In the same respect, do not shine your light before its time (i.e. the when). This will create a premature time of presentation; thusly, delaying or preventing you from winning. God's ways and timing are not our own. Learn to trust that His "when" is divinely connected to your "win." Only His way gets you the Gold and allows complete success and shine. Trust the when/win situations.

DAY 25

TODAY'S AFFIRMATIONS:

1. *I will never dim my light because I was created to shine.*
2. *My when is divinely connected to my win!*
3. *When God sanctions my when/win neither person nor adversity will hold me back.*
4. *My shine is a light I proudly emit in the hope to draw others to Christ.*
5. *I trust the when/win situations that God has set for my life. With Him, all I do is win, no matter the when.*

WRITE YOUR OWN DAILY AFFIRMATION:

Day 26

The WAIT

~ Psalms 25:3

You will not be put to shame for trusting in God…!

Waiting is not a typical virtue that people relish in. Each generation seems to create an object or concept to reduce the amount of time of process to production. However, we are all waiting and will have to wait on something in our lives. A lot of the discomfort with waiting is the unknown duration or the what if I missed God on something and am I waiting *without* because of it? Thusly, my waiting is essentially in vain.

One surety that Psalms 25:3 gives is you will not be put to shame for trusting in God. In other words, do not concern yourself with the length of time or even perceived mistakes, when you are following after God, He will ensure that you are not put to shame for trusting in Him while you wait on Him.

TODAY'S AFFIRMATIONS

1. I do not mind waiting on God.
2. When it comes to waiting on the Lord, I exude His Grace, determination, and trust.
3. Even if I have taken a wrong path, God has many paths and because I trust Him, I will not be disgraced (Proverbs 3:5-6).
4. I will NEVER be put to shame for trusting in God.

DAY 26

WRITE YOUR OWN DAILY AFFIRMATION:

Day 27

"Bit-by-Bit"

Luke 17:14

When he saw them, he said, "Go, show yourselves to the priests." And as they went, they were cleansed.

This is for the multi-talented, multi-gifted, and multi-called. This demographic is constantly bombarded with creativity, downloads from heaven, and a demand for their unique gifting. It is important that you understand, that organization of your day and thoughts will yield the greatest results. Women are generally multi-taskers but the aforementioned group has to learn to streamline what is needed for the day.

The Lord told me a while ago that even He did not create the world in one day. We have to learn to accomplish tasks bit-by-bit, until it is completed. Make the daily goal to work until it is done i.e. bit-by-bit. A financial advisor told me once to accomplish one task a week and by the end of the year, I would have 52 things accomplished! You do not want to be worn down when you do finally finish your daily tasks or monthly goals, get the wisdom of doing things bit-by-bit. The

Lord will honor your movement on a matter, and *as you go*, the Lord will perform on your behalf.

Also, after God worked to create for six days, He rested. Jesus is often noted dismissing the crowds or escaping to the mountains for downtime, which often followed moments where He had ministered to many people. After you work be sure to rest.

TODAY'S AFFIRMATIONS:

1. Like my Father, I am a creator with the ability to do many things. My movement is God-directed.
2. I have gained the wisdom of accomplishing daily tasks and goals bit-by-bit. Through this principle, I conquer both the small and the large.
3. Accomplishing one task is celebrated the same as finishing multiple goals.
4. I value me. Therefore, I take my day and the tasks within the day, bit-by-bit.
5. After my goal is complete, like my Father, I will rest.

WRITE YOUR OWN DAILY AFFIRMATION:

Day 28

"NOW"

John 9:4

I must work the works of Him who sent me while it is day; the night is coming when no one can work.

Live your life "a lot" today. Stop waiting for X amount of dollars, marriage, kids, house, certain career goals to be realized, for people to see your value, a certain person to apologize, for you to feel better or for you to "feel" like doing it. The greatest trick of the enemy is for us to believe we have more time. We do not know the day or the hour of the Lord's return nor do we know how many days we will ultimately have on this earth. WE have to work while it is day. The saved will not be judged on their sins, instead, we will be judged on our works.

How are you lining up?

Do it now. Whatever God has given your hands to do, do it today and do it with all your might!

In terms of production, allow the Lord to be your measure. People will look at some individuals and praise them for everything he or she has accomplished to date. However, this person may actually be behind the trajectory that the Lord has assigned for their hands. In other words, whatever God said you are to accomplish in a season is your goal not what man believes is best or deems to be enough. Oftentimes, people base what *you* can accomplish by what they believe *they* can do; as opposed to what the Lord has graced you for.

Fill in what has been deterring you _____. Decide today to leave it on the line and do not return.

DAY 28

TODAY'S AFFIRMATIONS:

1. I am working while it is day.
2. The Lord is my measure in determining what is too much or not enough for this season.
3. Everything I am created to do, I am doing it NOW!

WRITE YOUR OWN DAILY AFFIRMATION:

Day 29

"NEVER give up!"

Philippians 3:12-13

I know how to be abased, and I know how to abound. Everywhere and in all things I have learned both to be full and to be hungry, both to abound and to suffer need. I can do all things through Christ who strengthens me.

Vagaries, or the unexpected situations of life, can and will be taxing. The greatest of optimists will meet their day. There is a notion that only the strong survive. But, what makes the "truly" strong endure? They have grasped the balance in their minds of low and high times must be met with the same stratagem, Christ. I am not going to simply tell you that you need Jesus in order to experience the strength that verse 13 above states. I am going to tell you "how" to maintain strength during the toughest of moments and never give up!

First, you have to become *relentless in your pursuit of Christ*. If you have ever been in love with a man or discovered your passion, then likely there was a time that nothing or no one could keep you from him or it. Time spent, sometimes eating or sleeping did not matter all to engage with that person or to be in the presence of this new found love. Treat Jesus as this love but never let the flame burnout. Talk to Him daily, study Him, aim to please Him by loving what and who He loves. The return you get from Jesus loving you back will keep you in literal peace.

Next, *maintain your peace*. There are many clichés that encourage you to "protect your peace." However, I have witnessed some who implore all the boundaries, remove toxic things and people, drink plenty of water, mind their business, but yet these individuals still seem to lack peace. Why? True and total peace comes only from God. Philippians 4:6-8 shares how to maintain genuine peace. Verse 8 says that God's peace "surpasses" all understanding. This translates to when it would seem like you should give up and chaos has released all around you, you still have peace. Verse 8 lines out precept-by-precept how to have Godly peace and the last four words surmises it best; "**think** on these things." Your thought life controls the narrative of the health of your soul. Be sure to think on everything verse 8 describes. Here is a suggestion, keeping your mind on the things of God, His love, what He says about you, His purpose and plan for your life guarantees your peace in the midst of a storm. Do not allow your storms to cause you to give up!

Finally, *do not look back*. Self-reflection is a popular notion but I have found that people often turn that into retrospection, which ultimately leads to pity or nothingness. There are so many theories of Lot's wife looking back after the direct instructions not to (Genesis 19:26). There is nothing you can do with yesterday except take two L's. *Learn* from it and *leave* it! What I would like every reader to take away is your focus should be on the forward; nothing positive comes from dwelling on yesterday, press forward, and do not give up!

DAY 29

LIFE, people, enemies, your expectations, process to completion, sometimes friends or family may make you at least ponder giving up. Stopping is the only failure of life.

When we meet the Father on Judgment Day, Christ Believers will not be judged for sins but works. Work while it is day and no matter what, do not give up!

TODAY'S AFFIRMATIONS:

1. I will not live in the delusion that life does not carry ups and downs that I will have to balance in order to continually thrive.
2. I do not look back, only ahead. As it relates to my past, I know how to learn and how to leave.
3. I will never give up!
4. The only failure is stopping.
5. I live in a forward focus.
6. I pray everyday to maintain relationship with God.
7. Worship stills my souls while deepening the well of intimacy with the Lord that I draw from daily.

DAY 29

WRITE YOUR OWN DAILY AFFIRMATION:

Day 30

Chosen vs. Frozen

Luke 3:23

³Now Jesus himself was about thirty years old when he began his ministry. He was the son, so it was thought, of Joseph, the son of Heli,

This is for the woman that is getting unstuck. You may be familiar with the axiom, "when it rains, it pours." When rain comes, it often causes mud, decreased speed in traffic and overall makes it difficult (not impossible) to maneuver. If you have any familiarity with air travel, planes are still able to fly in the rain by rising above it. During the ascension above the rain, the plane may experience turbulence, but once above the storm, the plane will fly smoothly.

You are chosen to rise!

There are ways to get unstuck no matter the season of life "she" is in. God chose you for this life and He has a specific purpose. The first way you get unstuck is consistently **praying** to God. Prayer releases anxieties; it directs the burden to the one who cares, the only one that can make a true difference while simultaneously drawing you closer to Him. Secondly, remember why you are **chosen**. Rehearse and develop purpose in your mind and execute it throughout the day. If you are not aware of your purpose, refer back to step one and seek God until He makes it clear. Finally, remember you are chosen and *not frozen*. When something freezes it does not move. No matter what, keep going! One of my favorite sermons the Lord has given me to date is "Don't Shrink Back."

There are so many things that may make you feel inferior, stagnant or even dead. However, everyday, even in those moments, you have to choose to rise. Choose everyday to show up, get moving in your time with God and what He has instructed you to do. Eventually, you will get unstuck. The rain will come but remember you are chosen not frozen.

Day 30 for this journal was intentionally *chosen*. Many cultures, full adulthood is not attained until the age of 30. Jesus did not begin His public ministry until 30. Some religions do not allow individuals to begin leading in ministry until 30. The life season of 30 denotes maturity or full growth. For 30 days, you have received many affirmations and life tools to aid you in maturity or complete growth in your womanhood as H.E.R. Now that you have the tools to remain unstuck, remember you are not meant to survive but LIVE and THRIVE!

As noted, this journal was divinely designed with H.E.R. in mind. Every day was intentionally chosen, the words were Holy Ghost inspired and as you read every word and pronounced all the affirmations aloud, the Trinity affirmed the H.E.R. in you. Curses and inferiority were broken and the H.E.R. in you began to arise. Regardless of the season and what you are faced with today, woman, get moving! You are chosen.

DAY 30

TODAY'S AFFIRMATIONS:

1. I was chosen for God's divine purpose and plan.
2. I am fully developed in my God identity as *H.E.R.*
3. No person or designed hindrance will prevent me from living unstuck.
4. Today, I choose life!

WRITE YOUR OWN DAILY AFFIRMATION:

Day 31

I am God's Businesswoman

Luke 2:49

…Why did you seek Me? Did you not know that I must be about My Father's business?

Ending with Proverbs 31 may seem a little cliché; so, I'll end with Luke 2:49. But not before sharing a few things about the Proverbs 31 woman that you are. Proverbs 31 is a Queen Mother speaking to her future King son about the characteristics of the woman he should look for. Many of you may not be biological mothers, but as a woman you have learned the maternal, nurturing, and producing characteristics are innate to women of God. These characteristics are not limited in use for whom you may physically birth but they are for what and whom you are divinely assigned. There are many features of the Proverbs 31 woman but some of the highlights included her being an early riser (before her household), land purchaser, entrepreneur, resourceful and she is a place her man's heart could *trust* in. Proverbs 31 women hold financial value in the land, her money works for

H.E.R.; she is valuable to her family and community and overall trustworthy.

Women who have achieved this 31 day *Shift In Status* (SIS) understand that the woman described in Proverbs knows God and in turn knows herself and her value. SIS, you are no longer becoming but are H.E.R. affirmed.

> *Paralleling this book with Luke 2:49, essentially the Proverbs 31 woman is about the business of the Father.*

Today's journal is your official graduation day! You have obtained the necessary tools to know, grow and glow in the things of God. Today and the remainder of all your days, may you be about the Father's business. When people find or look for you, let them catch you working!

You are about the Father's business…

God's Businesswoman to be exact.

Everything does not have to be totally developed today.

You are **H.E.R.**

You are Heaven en Route…

May you be fully received in His identity for you and if not you will now see the rejection as God's protection!

LIVE and THRIVE Queens!

TODAY'S AFFIRMATIONS:

1. I am H.E.R.!!! Everything may not be there, but by God's grace, I am Heaven en Route and everyone will see HIM through me!

2. I am God's Businesswoman as daily; I am about my Father's business.

3. Today, I do not survive but choose to LIVE and THRIVE!

WRITE YOUR OWN DAILY AFFIRMATION:

Closing Thoughts

I believe this journal did and will continually do all God purposed for it. These LIFETIME affirmations and words will make literal moves in your life to keep with the spurred production and never being stuck. Keep affirming and calling H.E.R. forward!

Ebony D. Green

Ebony Green is the founder and CEO of Business and Books, LLC and a proud South Carolina native. Business and Books, LLC has helped numerous Christian schools, authors, ministries and entrepreneurs (S.A.M.E.) market and brand God's way through the company's brand, Market ME –God™. Business and Books, LLC promotes unity in the Body of Christ and the marketplace with their app, The KINGdom Directory (available on Google Play store).

Ebony has pegged herself as "God's Businesswoman ™." Similar to the company's motto, she is all about the Father's business. Her education includes an undergraduate degree in English-Literature. A Masters of Education in Early Childhood and Childhood Education, and a Juris Doctor degree. In 2019, the U.S. Commission on Civil Rights appointed her to a four-year term for the S.C. Advisory Committee Board. She is also one of The 2019 Whole Truth Magazine's 40 under 40.

In addition to business, Ebony is also a licensed minister and is affirmed to the office of the Prophet. Her personal ministry is "Hands and Feet Ministries ~ Breaking the Walls of Tradition." She is also the founder of Make Things Move Campaign, a prayer line for Christ believing women. For booking, please email booking@businessbooksllc.com.

www.ingramcontent.com/pod-product-compliance
Lightning Source LLC
Chambersburg PA
CBHW071223090426
42736CB00014B/2948